FUTURE FANTASTIC
21st Century Digital Art

George Walters

George Walters
1005 Market St, Ste 408
San Francisco, CA 94103-1627

415.861.3918

Gwalters415@yahoo.com

Published
August, 2010

CONTENTS

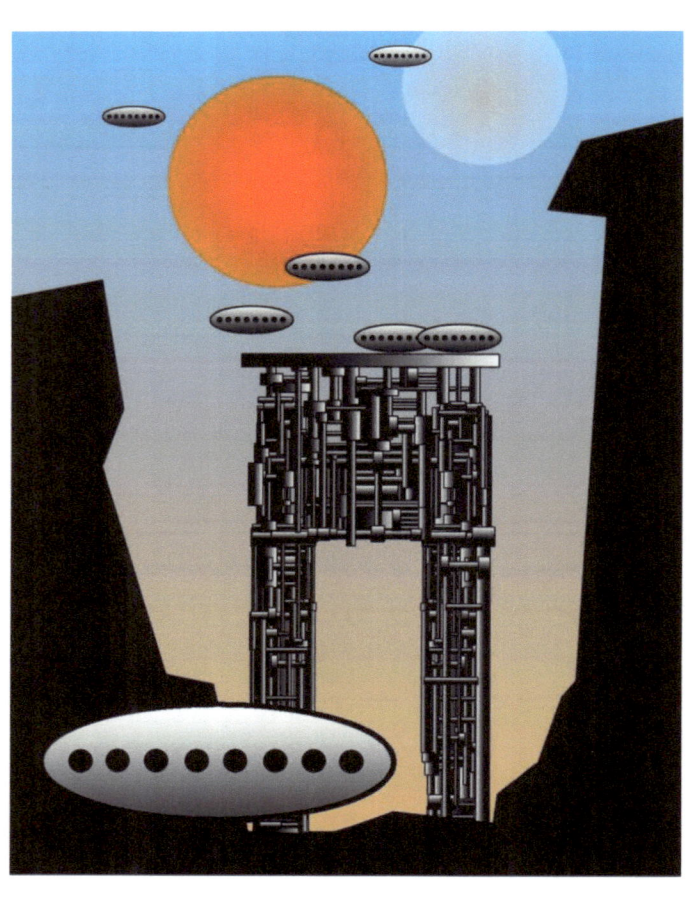

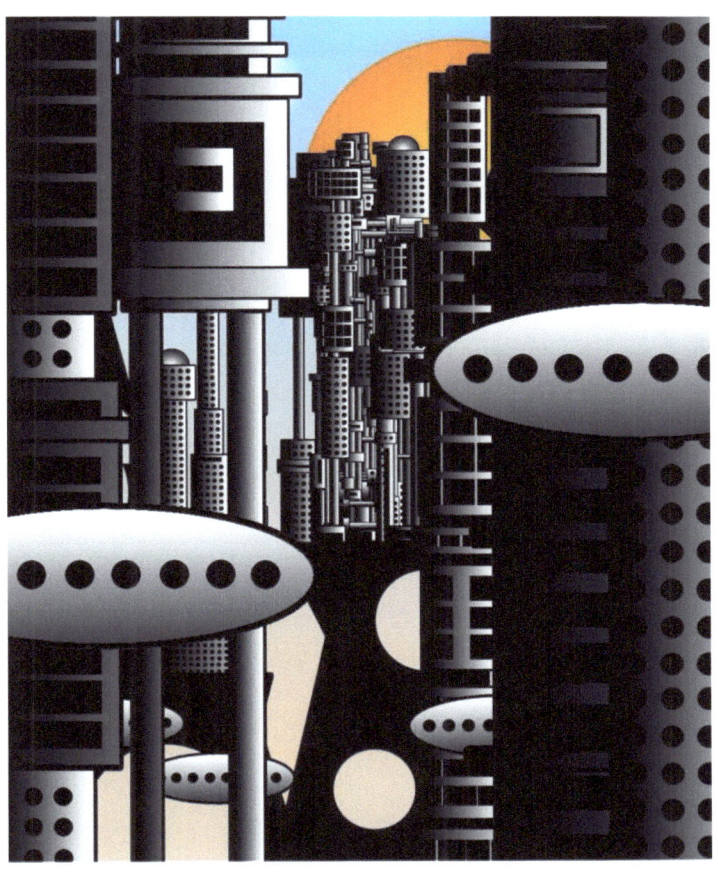

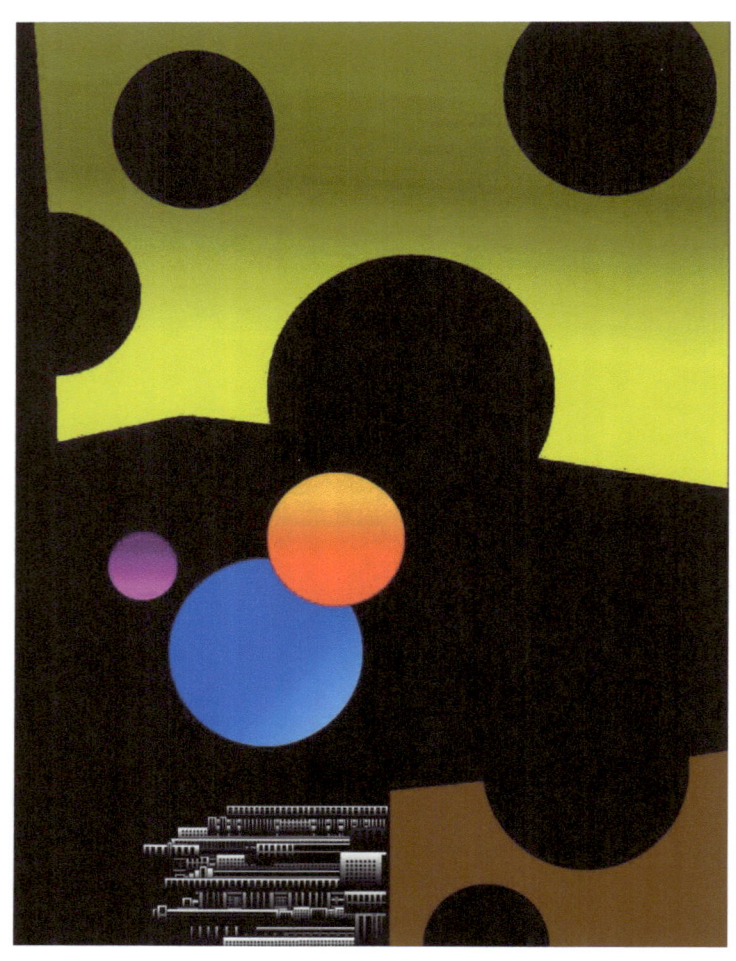

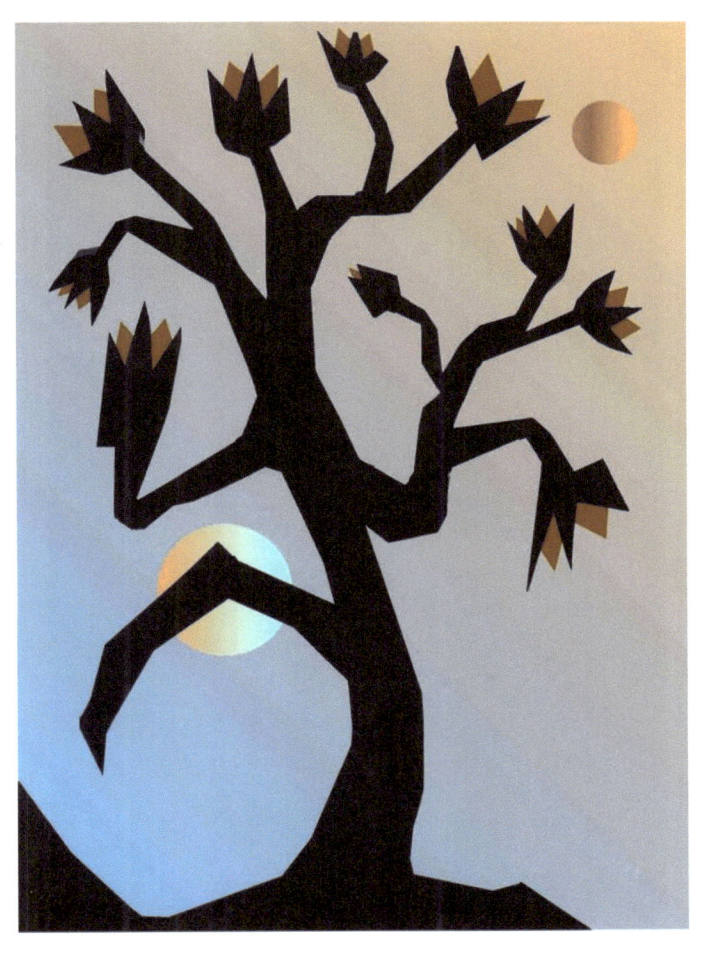

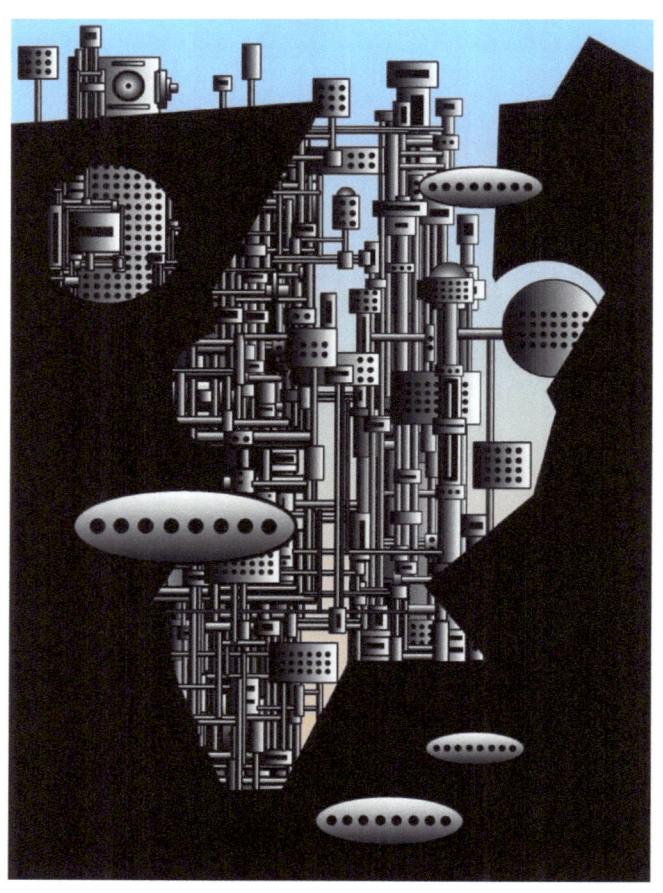

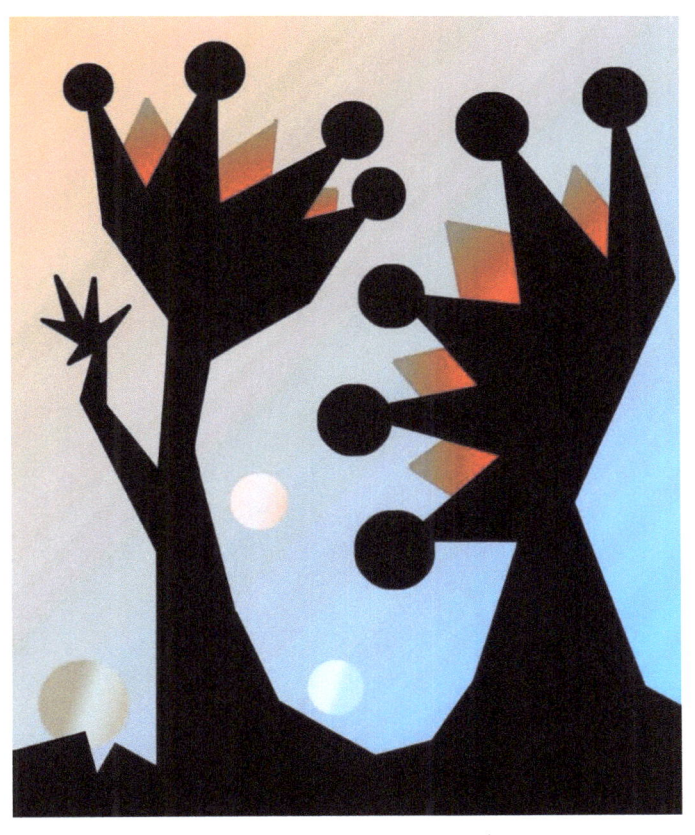

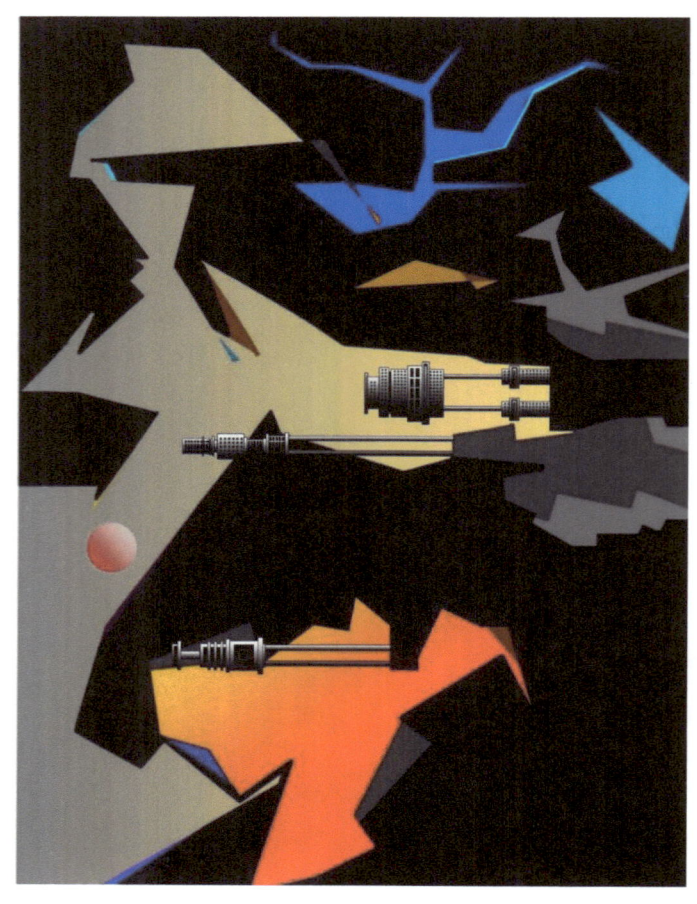

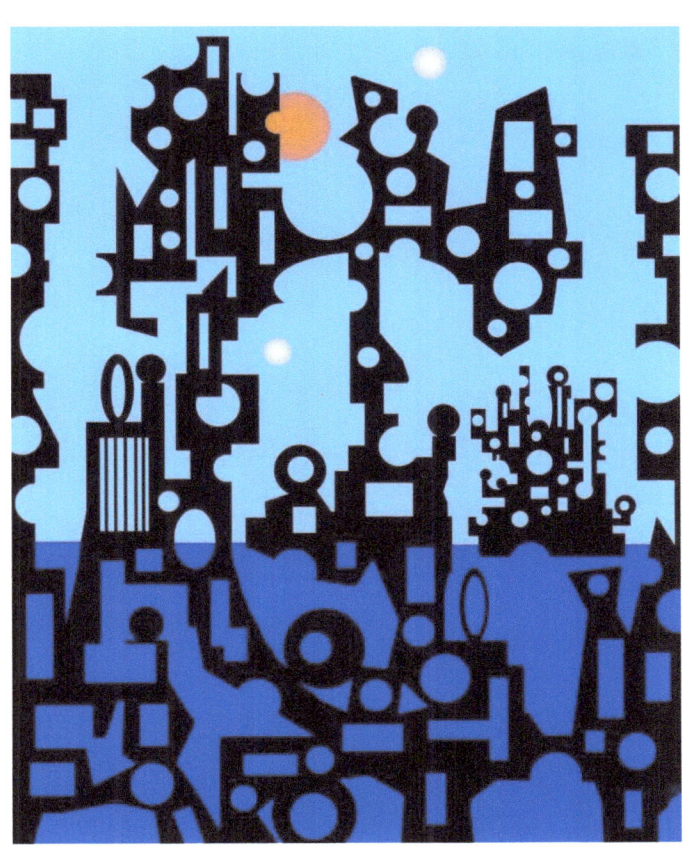

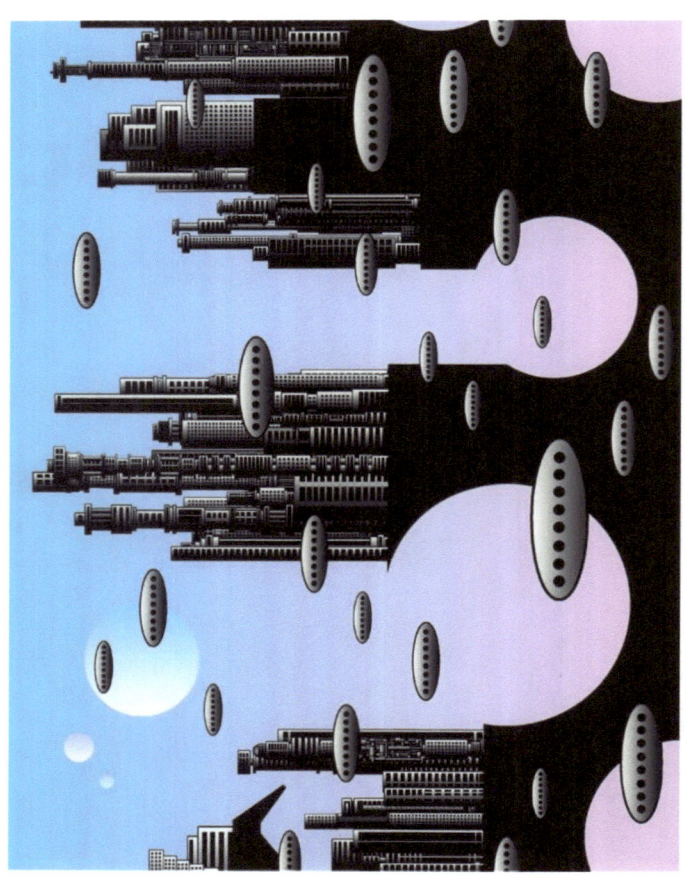

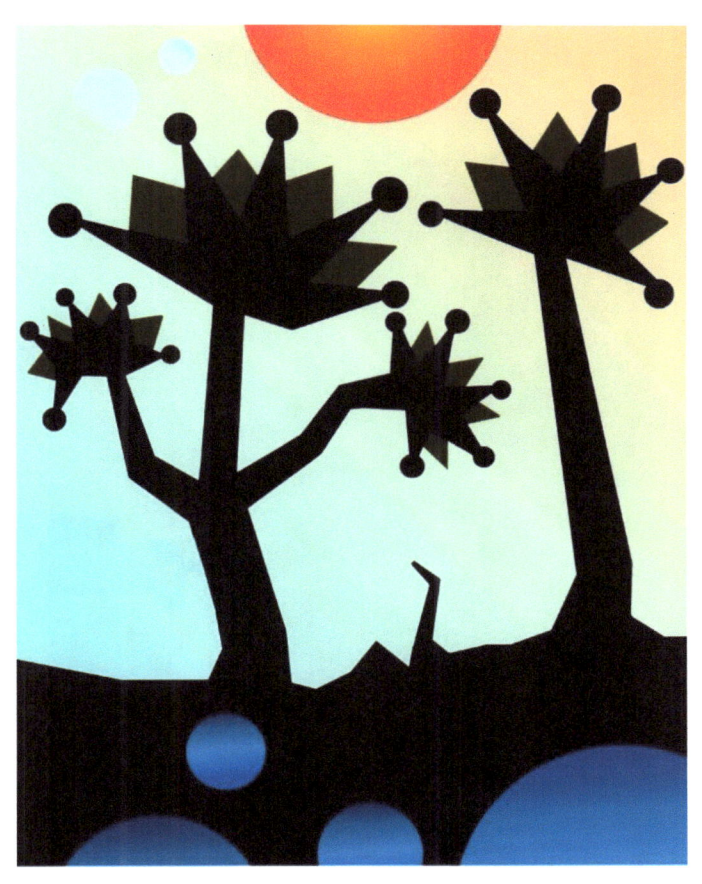

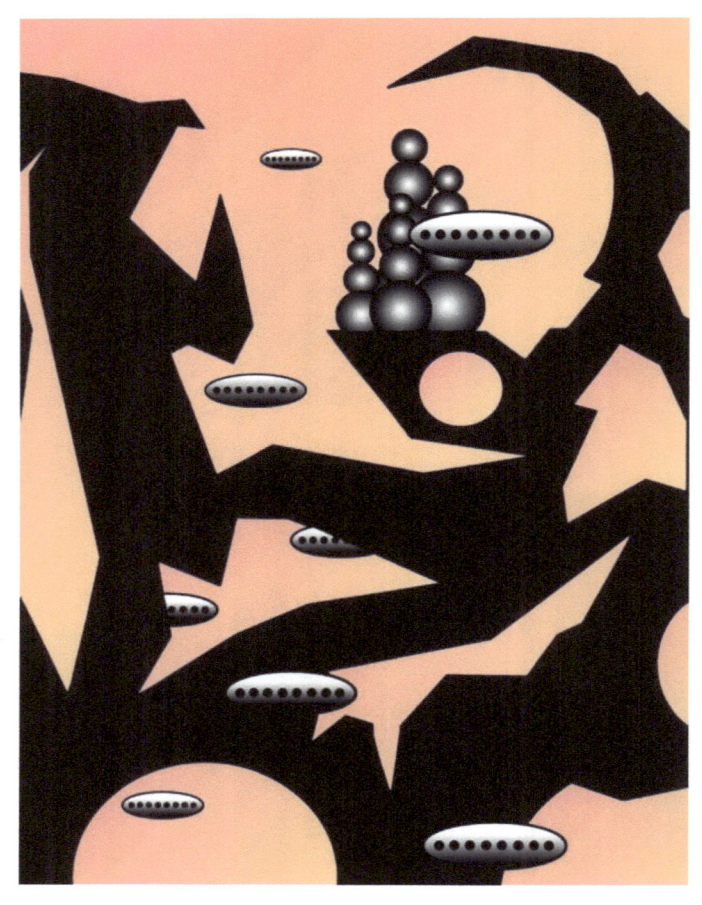

14

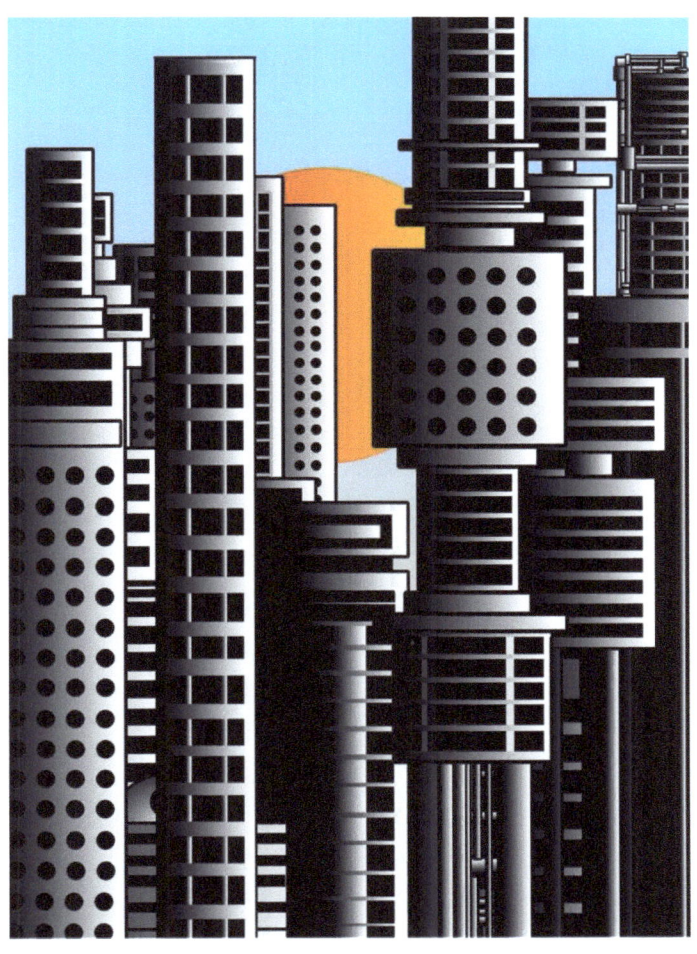

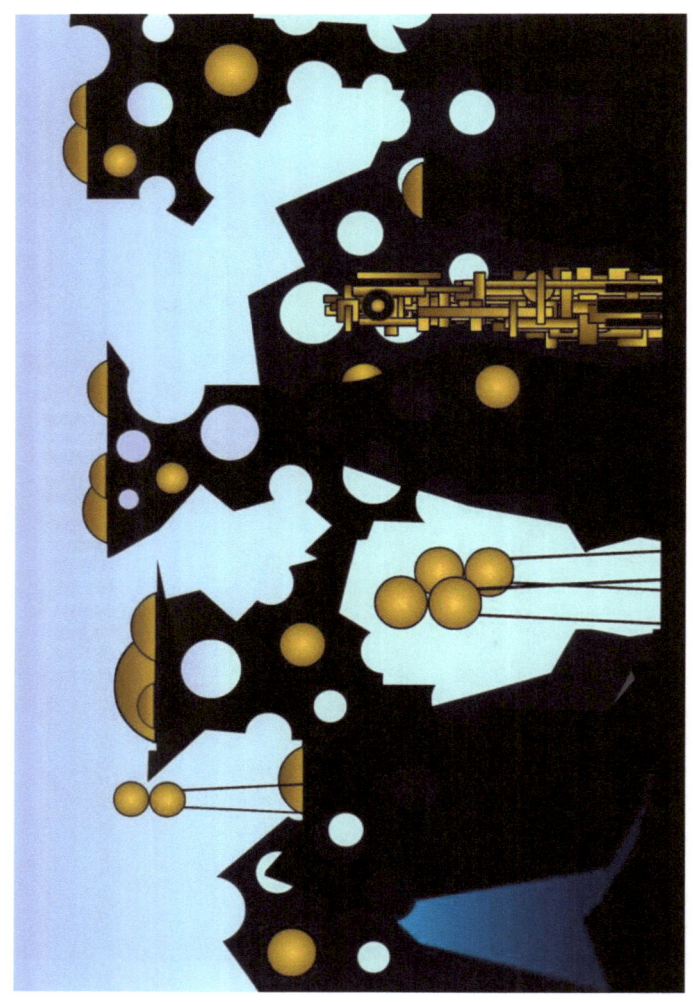

16

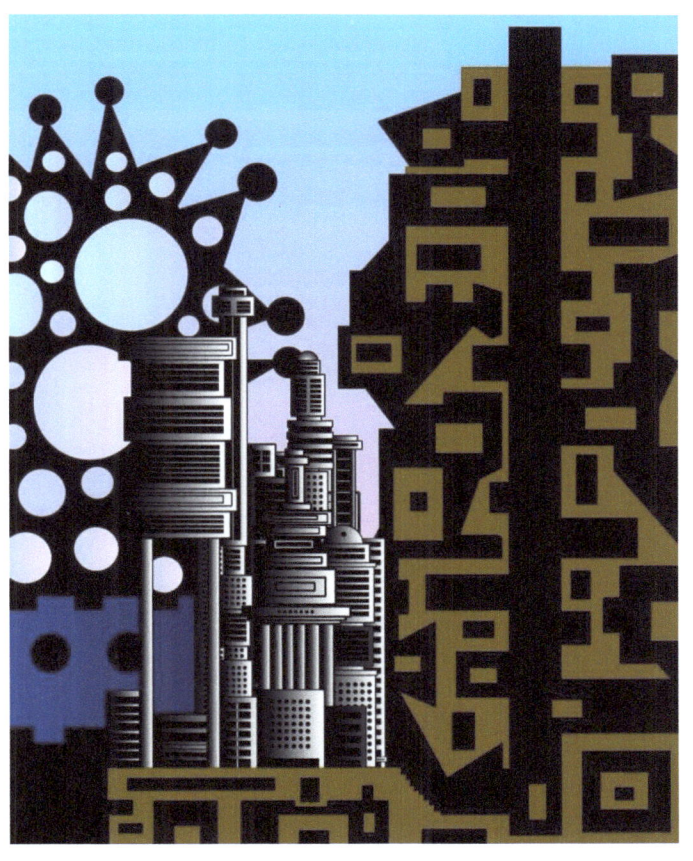

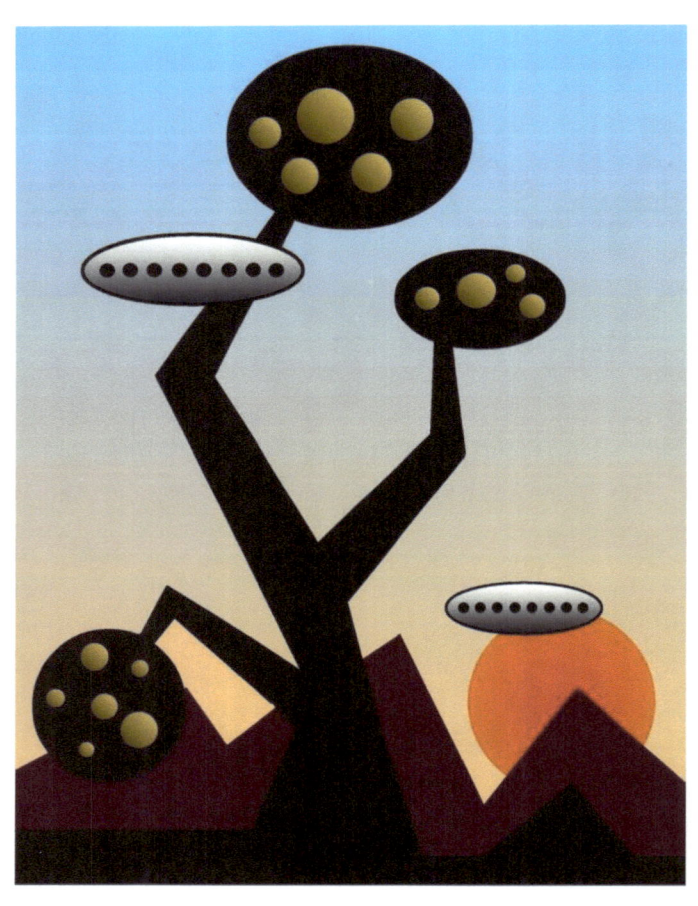

18

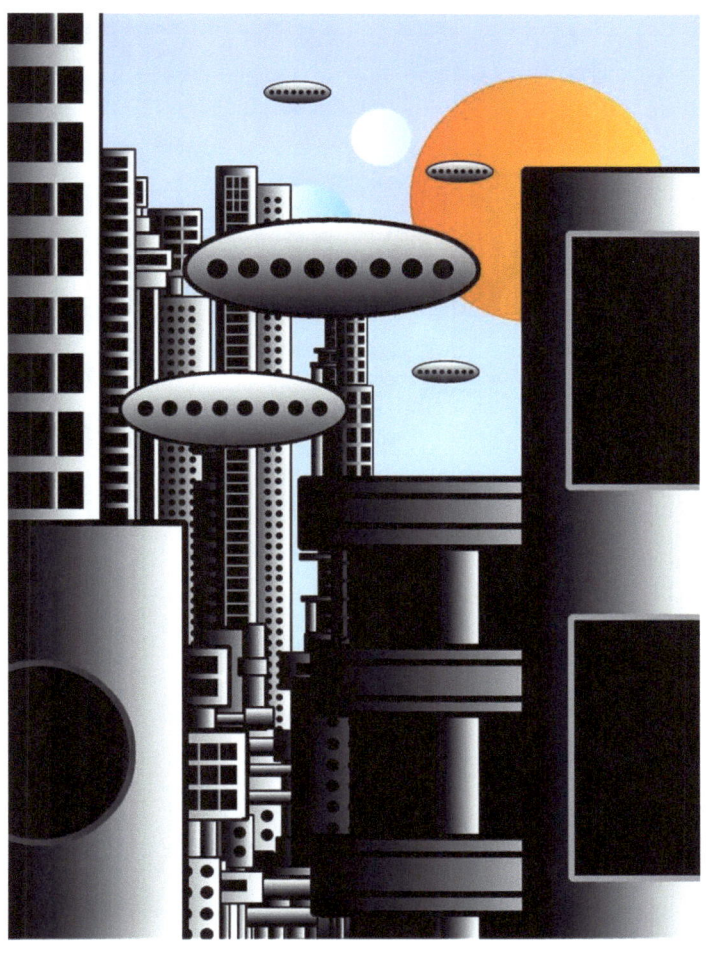

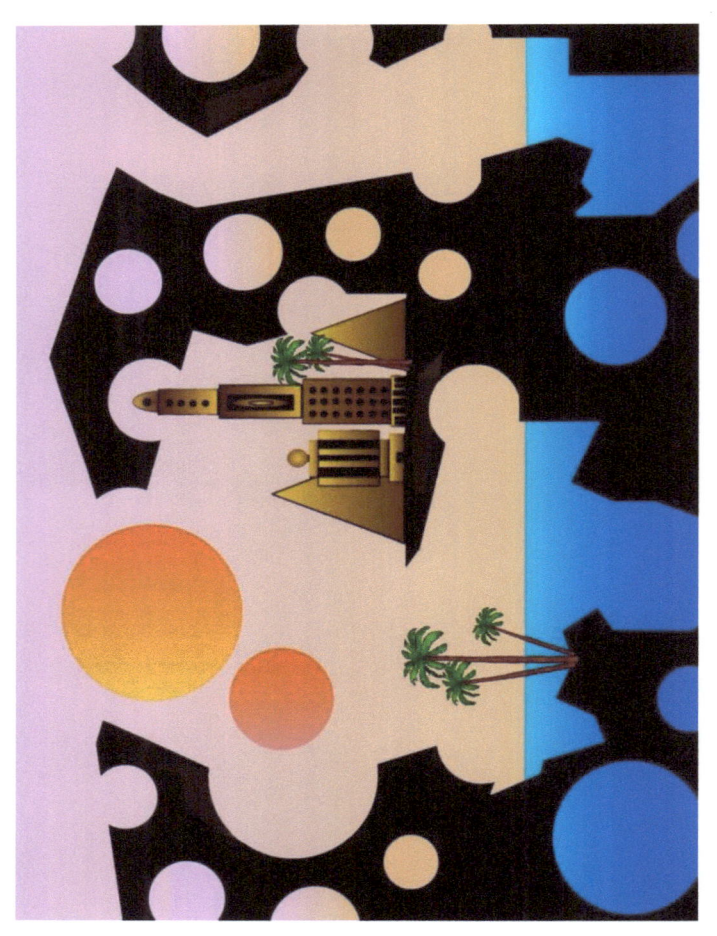

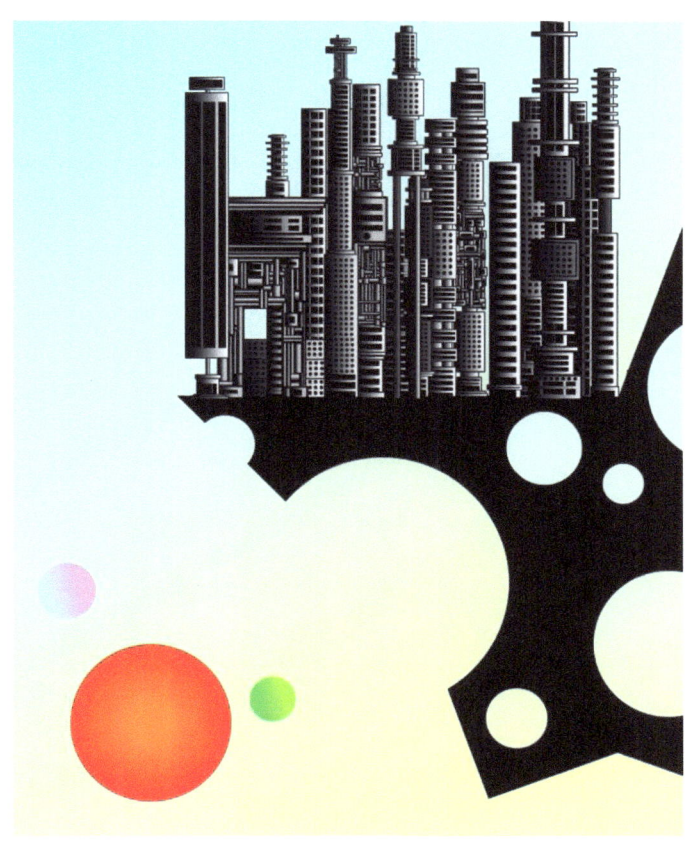

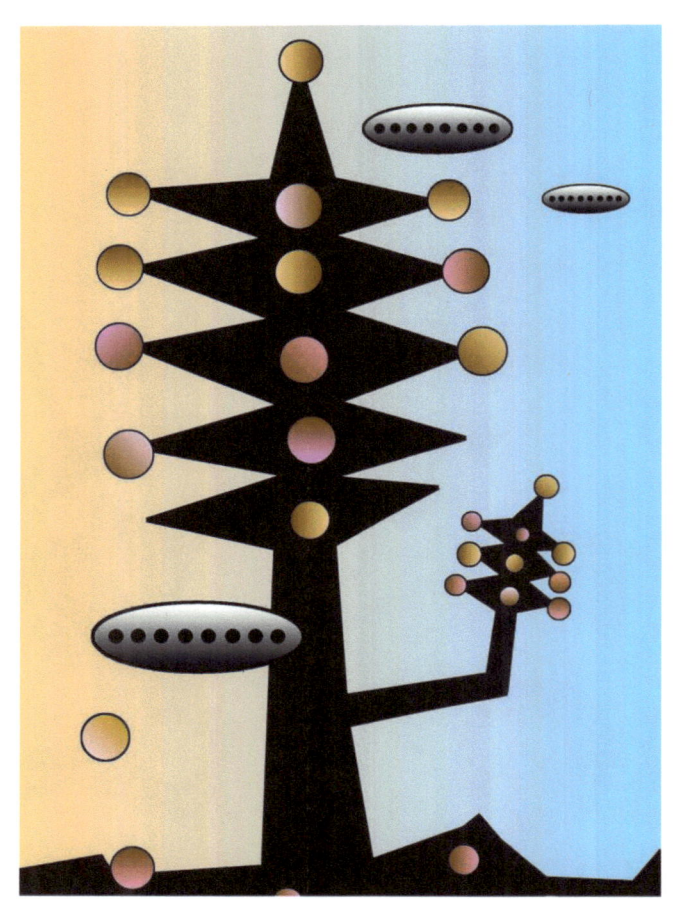

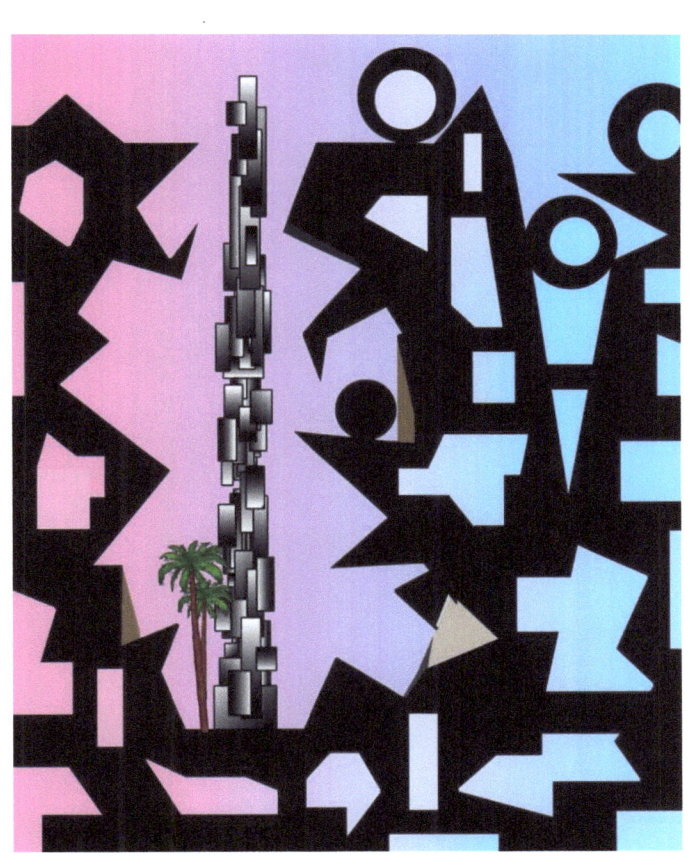

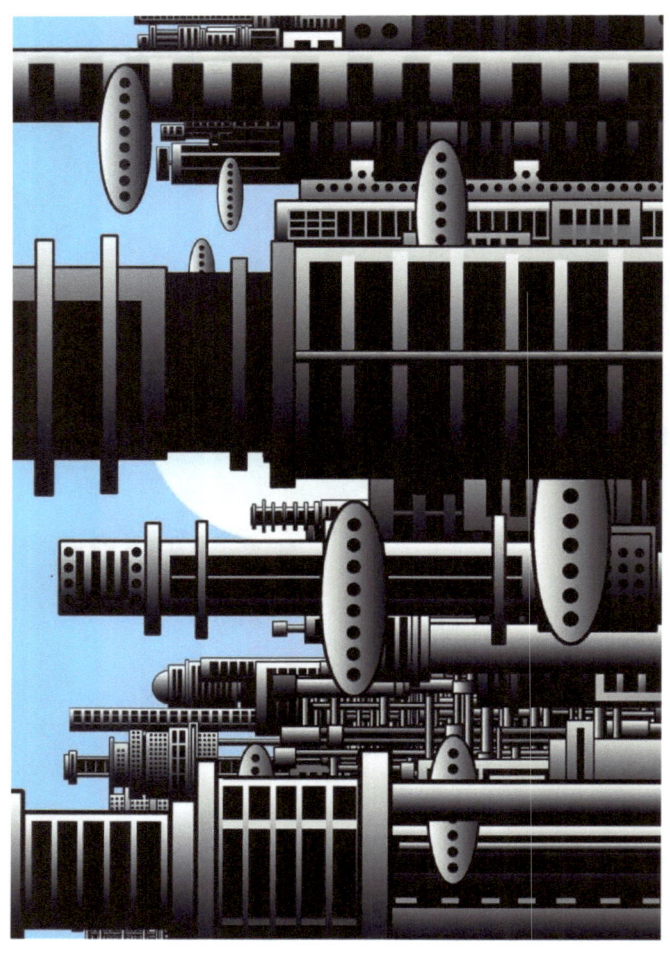

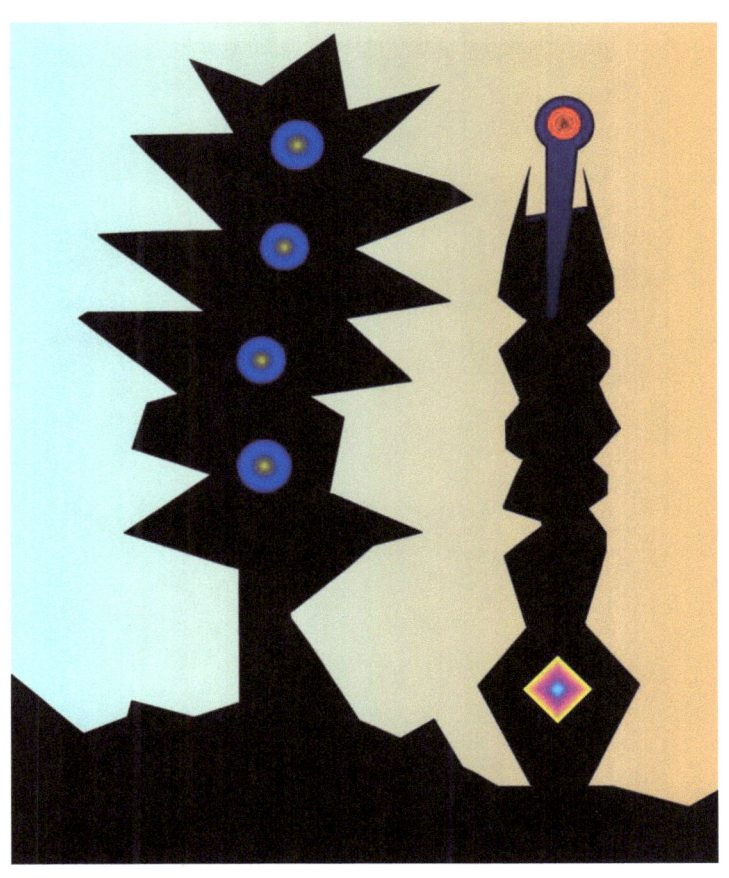

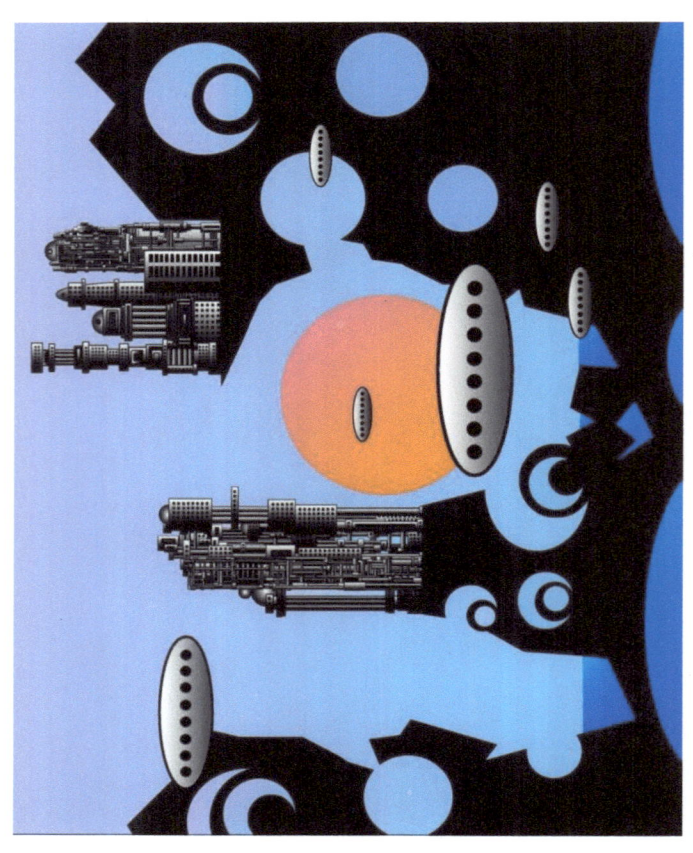

26

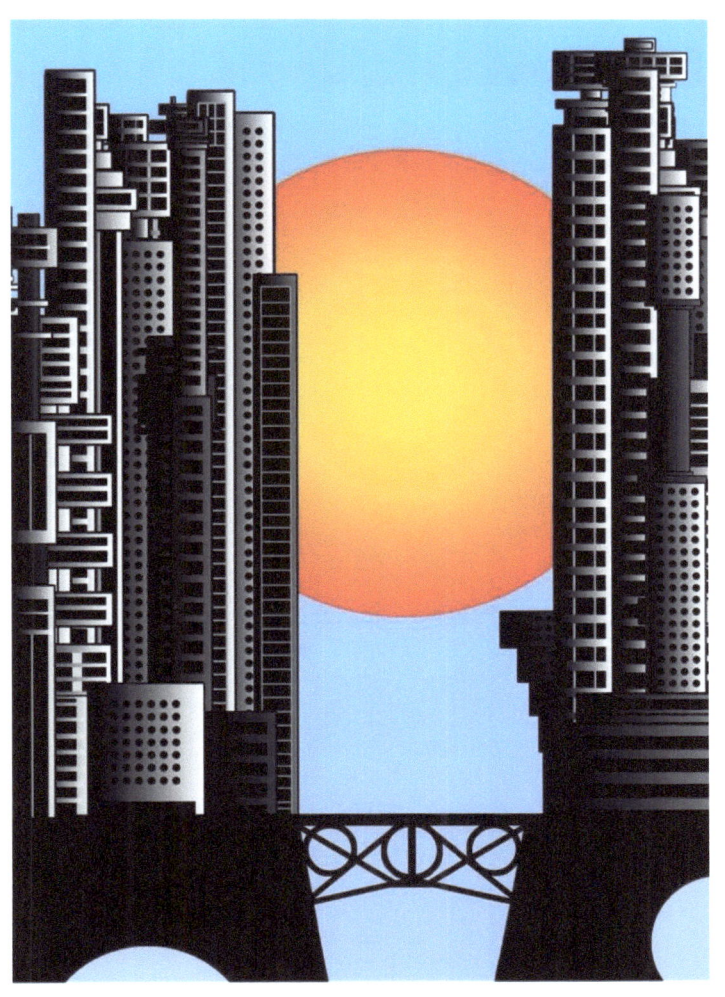

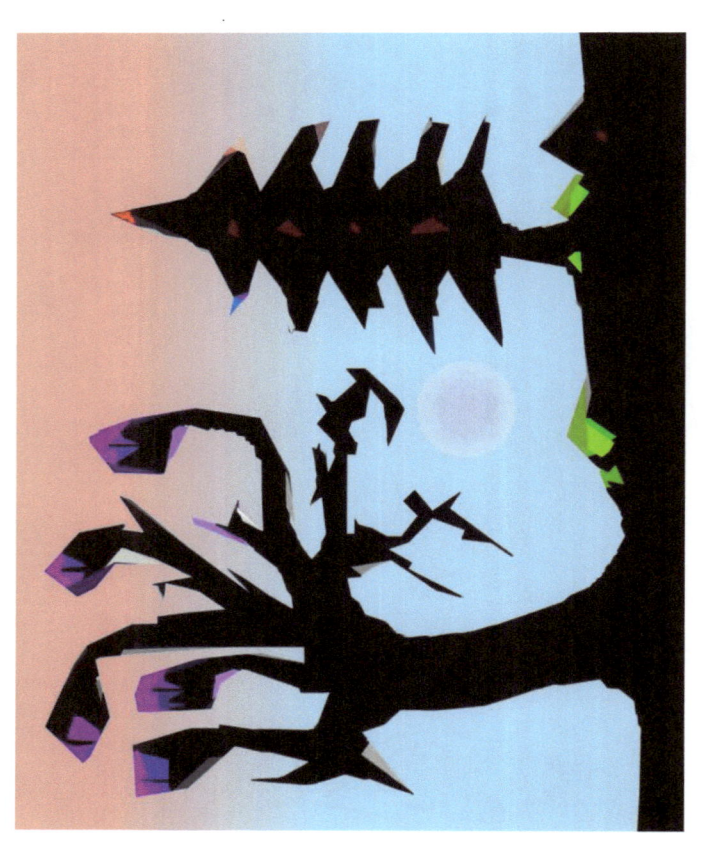

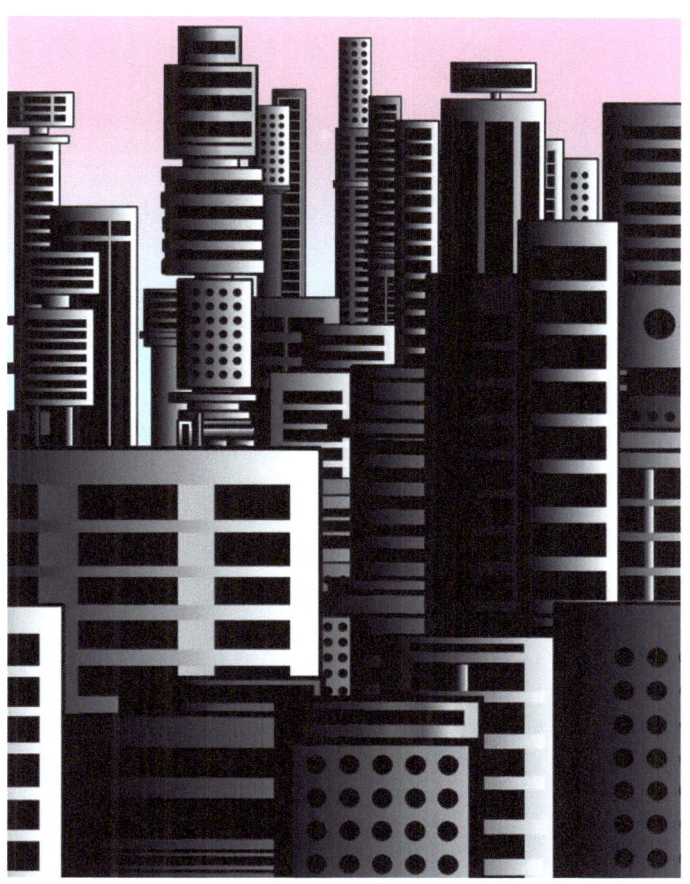

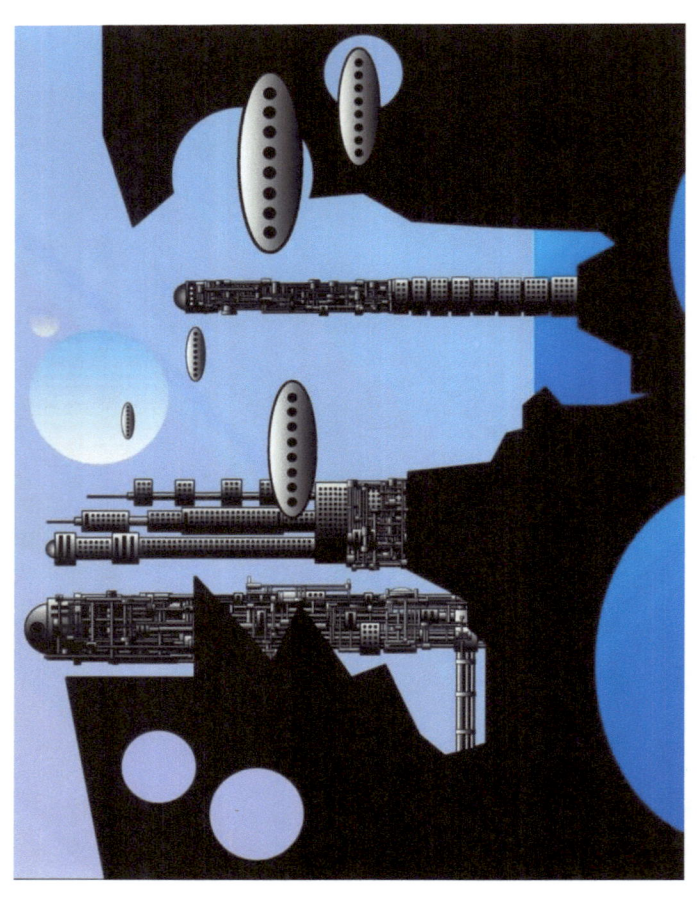

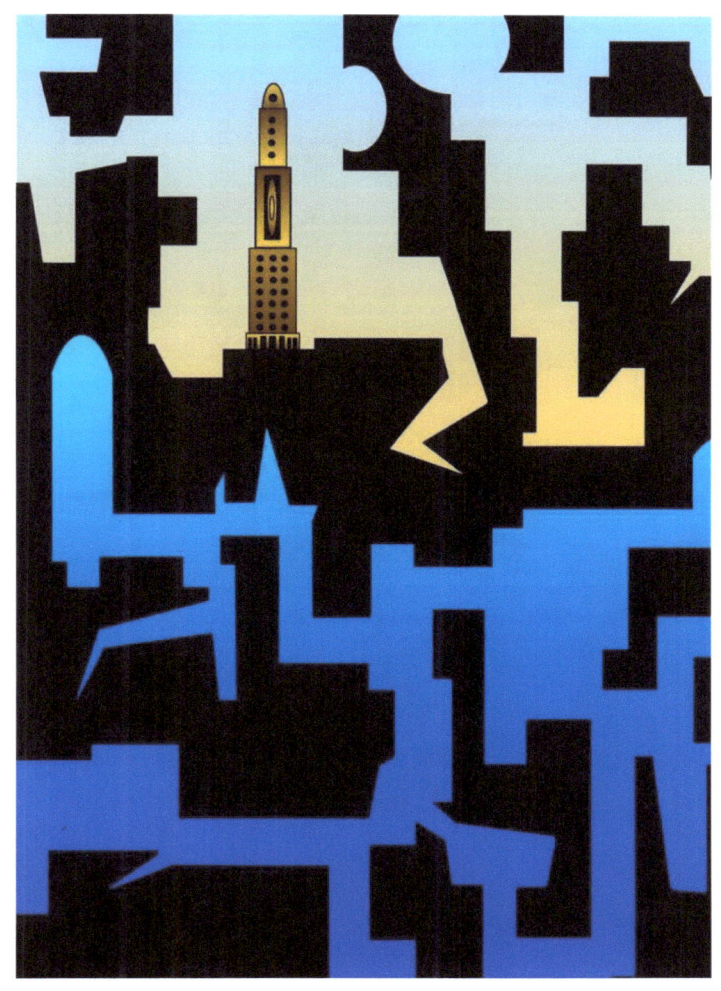

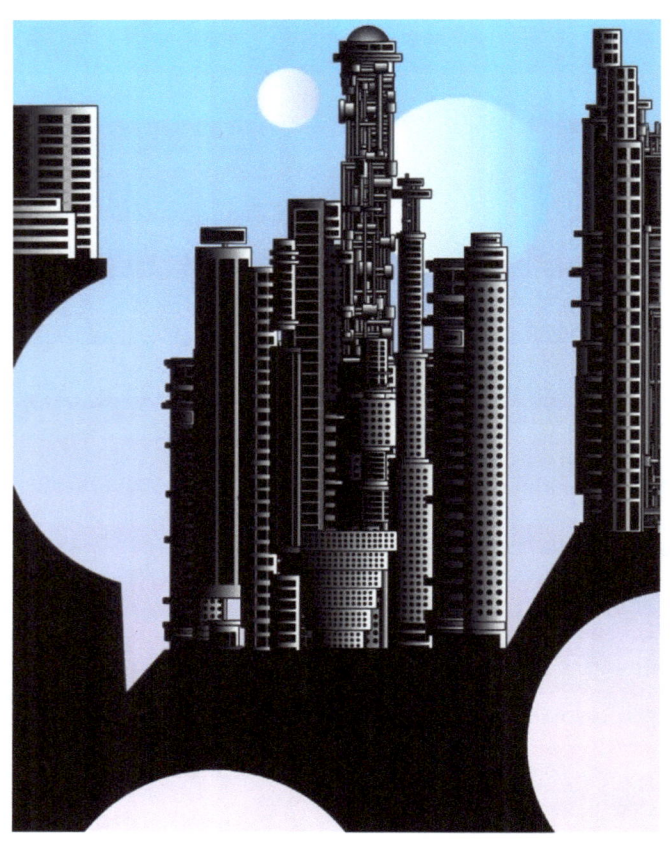

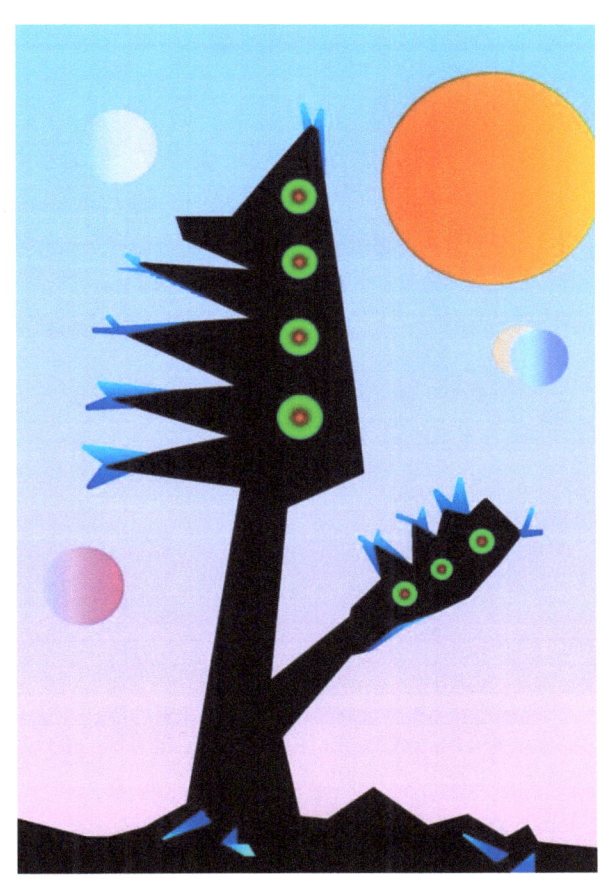

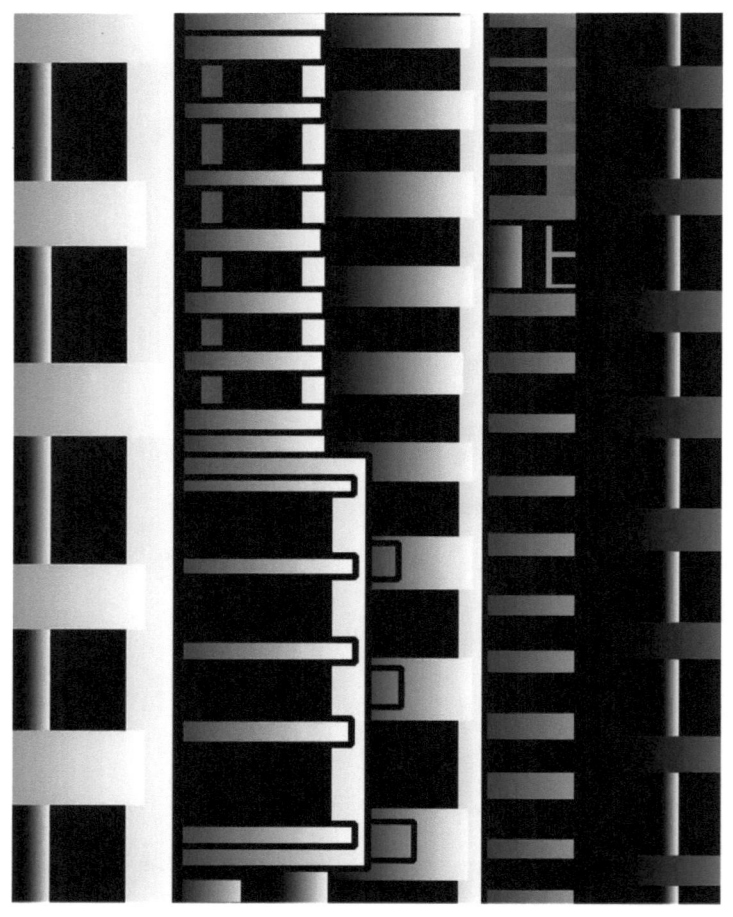

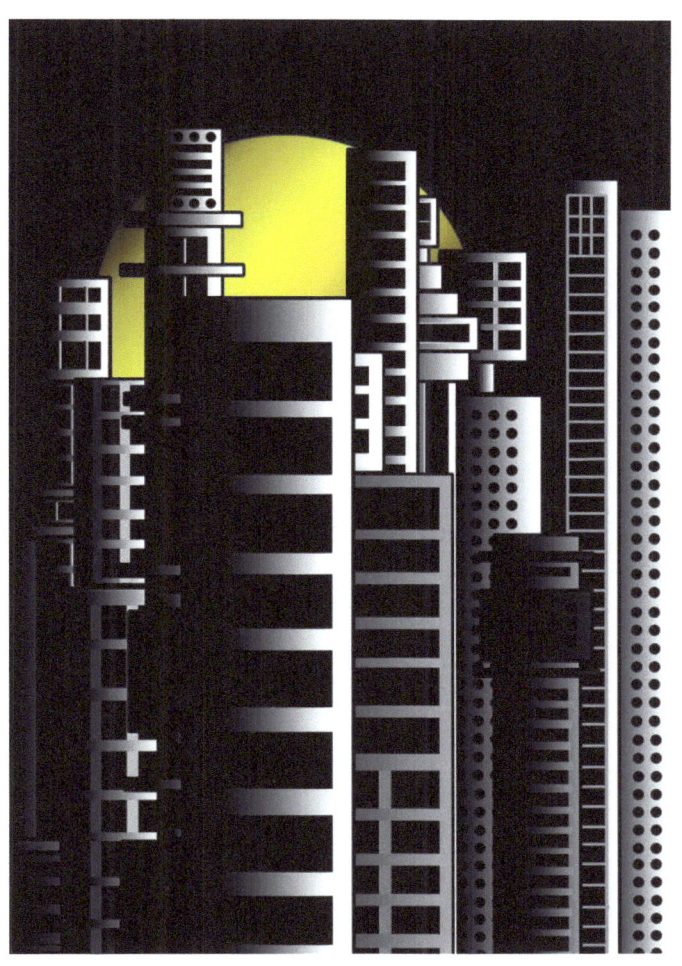

ACKNOWLEDGEMENTS

I would like to express my sincere appreciation and gratitude to Alfredo Garcia-Lucio, Anthony Evec, Arthur Childs, Arthur Ramirez, Ben McDonald, Bernard Cummings Jr, Brett Troxell, Christopher Arnold, Christian Laird, Conrad Hechter-Heyns, Damien Grey, Daniel Detorie, Daniel Nicoletta, Daniel Tousignant, Dave Bowman, Dave Peterson, David Fink, David Hughes, David Strickland, Dennis Hall, Derek Spreckelmyer, Derrick Sands, Diego Taborda, Don Baird, Don Ross, Giovanni Arrighi, James Scott Geras, Jedd Garet, Jen Ole Krause, John Major, Jose Mineros, Justin Bond, Kevin Cata, Kevin McGrath, Kurt Bauer, Kyle Harney, Kym Kleiman, Leonard Perillo, Marc Calderon, Mark Paron, Mark Sink, Matthew Beals, Mica Billings, Michael Blue, Michael Holland, Michael Purcell, Nathan Butler, Nicholas Yankosky, Nikki Rivera, Paul Alley, Paul Courey, Phil Sloan, Randy Bard, Randy Roberts, Randy Webb, Raven Ashley, Rob Young, Rocky Lane, Ronald Crawford, Sonya Wagoner, Stephen Duddy, Steve Lewis, Thomas Barnes, Thomas Scott, Todd Ditto and Tony Cartwright for their unconditional friendship, support and or words of encouragement over the years.

You guys rock!

www.ingramcontent.com/pod-product-compliance
Lightning Source LLC
Chambersburg PA
CBHW041147180526
45159CB00002BB/744